a morning cup of prayer® for teachers

FaithPoint PRESS

This edition published for FaithPoint Press by arrangement with Crane Hill Publishers.

ISBN-13: 978-1-58173-597-0
ISBN-10: 1-58173-597-9

Book design by Miles G. Parsons
Illustrations by Tim Rocks and Christena Brooks
Cover art by Christena Brooks

Printed in China

a morning cup of prayer®
for teachers

A daily guided devotional for a lifetime of inspiration and peace

john a. bright-fey

FaithPoint™ PRESS

Acknowledgments

I would like to thank the following individuals for their invaluable help and advice. This Morning Cup would surely not taste as sweet without their assistance:

To Professor Tom Gibbs for talking me into teaching college classes on prayer and contemplative living;
To all of my students whose experience of prayer and faith has profoundly moved me and deeply informed my work;
To Ellen, Linda, and all the staff and artists at Crane Hill Publishers for giving me this glorious opportunity;
To my amazing wife, Kim, who helps me in more ways than she could possibly know;
To the many men and women of faith that have, through the years, guided and shaped my life of prayer.

I thank God for each of you.

Dedication

In Loving Memory
Viola Gertrude Patricia Caverlee Marshall
"Grandma Vi"

Thanks for teaching me how to listen.

Contents

This is the confidence we have in approaching God: that if we ask anything according to his will, he hears us. And if we know that he hears us—whatever we ask—we know that we have what we asked of him.

—1 John 5:14-15

Foreword

Would you, as a teacher, like closer contact with God? If your answer is "Yes," then this book was written for you. With it, you can begin an incredible journey into the heart of God, and come to know Him as never before. The means to begin this journey, and the power to sustain it for a lifetime are the same: prayer.

Part devotional and part instruction manual, this *Morning Cup of Prayer* is designed to be a spiritual patchwork quilt of advice, wisdom, and inspiration. With it, you will find peace with God as you surrender to His love through prayer.

I've tried to write this book so that you will be able to absorb its contents easily. Feel free to approach it in whatever way you find most satisfying. As you give it your attention, consider it within the context of your own career, devotional path, and religious life.

I say that "I wrote" this book, but in truth, my hand was guided by God and its contents formed by His Grace. I felt His love with every word. Now, it is my sincerest wish that you feel it, too.

Teachers and Prayer

For most of my life I have been a teacher. There have been so many situations in my own teaching life that have sent me to my knees in prayer to ask for guidance and grace. Knowing firsthand the tremendous needs of teachers, it has never ceased to amaze me just how many of my colleagues, simply, do not pray.

It makes me sad and, truthfully, leaves me more than a little bewildered. The problems encountered by today's teachers, frankly, cry out for prayer. To my way of thinking, that's how it should be.

Prayer can change the course of an individual life or the life of a nation. Families torn apart by strife, disaster, or indifference can be made whole again with prayer. It can cure the worst physical illnesses and heal the deepest emotional wounds. If we become lost, it helps us to find our way again.

Prayer knows. It pulls us back from the brink of what is toxic and shows us where and when to move forward towards nourishment. Most importantly, prayer is our birthright as God's children. It energizes, strengthens, comforts, informs, supports, and protects us. Simply put, prayer reclaims lives, futures, and souls. I truly believe it can inspire students, guide teachers, and cure what ails our schools.

With all that prayer has to offer, why then don't more teachers pray? The answer is simple: they don't know how. As strange as that answer might sound, whenever I've asked the question of teachers, "Do you pray?" it's the response that I am most likely to receive.

Perhaps you are one of those teachers who needs the complete wholeness that prayer provides but find yourself confused about the subject. Maybe the stresses of your job keep you so busy that you just don't know how, when, or where to pray. The book you are now holding will solve those problems. It will help clear the path and show you the way to prayer.

I've divided this book into roughly three parts. The first will be a discussion of the special needs of teachers that can be addressed by prayer. We have the greatest example of a teacher in our Savior Jesus Christ. His lessons were direct and to the point. He loved all of His students equally and used marvelous parables to illustrate His lessons. When people addressed Him as Rabbi they were saying, "My Teacher." Indeed, as teachers we have tall shoes to fill.

So many teachers today face near insurmountable obstacles in their careers. You can become so completely mired in the conflicts and complexities of teaching in a modern world, that you lose touch with your inspiration. You often forget why you became a teacher in the first place. The key to remembering those reasons, being inspired, and becoming the best teacher you can possibly be is prayer.

The second part of this book will be a discussion of the mechanics of prayer and some of its methods. I will also discuss what a prayerful life can look like.

Most often, when someone tells me, "I don't pray," what they are really saying is, "I don't know what to say to God." If you are one of those individuals, please don't worry. In the third part of this book, I will present you with an assortment of Biblically based prayers and relevant passages from His Word that both support and augment them.

Each scriptural prayer was written especially to address the needs of teachers. They are grouped with scripture passages that every teacher should find suitable for contemplation and prayer. Take your time when reading them as they contain much food for thought.

Please look upon these prayers as suggestions. True prayer is a profoundly personal thing that must come from your heart. Think of the prayers and passages in this book as starting points for your personal spiritual journey. Use them to get comfortable with the act of praying. Then, as guided by the Holy Spirit, you will learn to speak the language of prayer.

In the time it would take for you to have a pleasant cup of tea before your first class of the day, you can begin your spiritual journey and sustain it for a lifetime. I believe that heartfelt prayer is the teacher's elixir of life that, once tasted, changes our teaching lives for the better. More importantly, it changes our students' lives as well. Would you like to share a Morning Cup with me?

JBF
Birmingham, Alabama
2006

The fear of the LORD is the beginning of wisdom;
all who follow his precepts have good understanding.
To him belongs eternal praise.
—Psalm 111:10

Why Teachers Need Prayer

Teachers, by anyone's estimation, have one of the most important jobs a person can have. Indeed, most would tell you that teaching isn't a job to them; it's a calling. That's how it should be.

Teaching shapes and secures the generations yet to be. Teachers mold the futures of individuals, families, cultures, and countries. They accomplish this through the imparting of knowledge and by setting a good example. You'd think that the decision to shoulder this responsibility, would garner teachers more help and respect. But all too often, they just don't get it.

As teachers, we are confronted with many challenges and trials that have nothing to do with the imparting of knowledge. And each of those issues has the potential of being either a minor annoyance or something so serious that it can destroy a career. Teachers must learn to be fearless and surge forward. At the same time, they must also learn when it is appropriate to restrain themselves or even withdraw.

Teachers are warriors one minute and servants the next. They must be dreamers and pragmatists, simultaneously. Most importantly, they have to be students themselves continually involved in a silent game of call and response, weighing what they know against new situations and circumstances.

Said another way, any teacher worthy of the name is responsible for recreating themselves each and every day. To some, this may sound like an impossible task. But God sent His only Son to save us and, in doing so, He put the impossible within our reach.

I believe that, when guided by the Holy Spirit, each of us knows full well the extent of our gifts and our deficits. We intrinsically know what to do to conquer our fears and address those issues that stand between us and our being the person God knows us to be. We have but to do it.

But what are the issues confronting today's teachers? What are those problems and situations that the gift of prayer can address?

Here is a partial list:

- Feeling overworked and overwhelmed
- Being a good role model
- Budget shortfalls and under funding
- Overcrowded classrooms
- Learning to care for your students while still caring for yourself
- Learning when and how to be a disciplinarian
- Dealing with an incompetent or indifferent administration
- Recognizing students who are victims of abuse
- School violence
- Losing touch with personal career goals
- Losing passion for teaching
- Being a "Superteacher" who can do anything
- Feeling trapped
- Dealing with bureaucracy and red tape
- Letting yourself have fun in the classroom
- Changes in administration
- Changes in teaching standards and requirements
- Feeling isolated and abandoned
- Being who you really are
- Futility
- Depression
- Anger
- Feeling taken for granted
- Feeling alone
- Feeling tired

Surely, I could continue, but these issues seem to be the ones that most teachers face day-to-day. Perhaps you have experienced one or more of these conditions in your teaching life. Perhaps you are experiencing them now. If you are, then it's time to take the key of prayer and through Christ Jesus enter your Father's house to seek His wisdom. If you can pray authentically, that is from your heart, then you will be shown how to overcome these or any problems. It's as simple as that.

And I will do whatever you ask in my name, so that the Son may bring glory to the Father. You may ask me for anything in my name, and I will do it.
—John 14: 13-14

What Is Prayer?

Let's approach this as educators. The stated goal of this book is to teach you to pray. In order to do that, we need a definition of precisely what "praying" is. We also need to discuss the different kinds of prayer and the best ways to approach them. Before we get much further, though, I have a story about a wonderful teacher in my own life. I think it will help us get things off to a good start and insure a great finish.

A Teacher's Example of Prayer

My inspiration for this book on prayer and the model I use for conducting a prayerful life come from a teacher that was—and is—very near and dear to my heart.

Everything I know about prayer I learned from my maternal grandmother, Viola. Grandma Vi was a devout churchgoer and easily the most amazing Christian that you'd ever be likely to meet. To be fair, I've learned a lot about prayer, contemplation, and devotion from many other wonderful men and women of faith. But the lessons from Grandma remain to this day the most profound, direct, and the most useful that I've ever received. Everything she did—whether it was homemaking, teaching music, comforting a friend or being a wife and grandmother—she approached with prayer.

Every morning after putting away the breakfast dishes, Grandma Vi would quietly announce that she was going to her room to "talk with God." She would then retire to the back bedroom, close the door, and do precisely that. Forty-five minutes to an hour later, she would emerge renewed, refreshed—transformed really—confident, self assured, and positively radiant.

No matter what difficulties life presented her, the negative would literally fade away as her smile and countenance pushed back the gloom. The grace she radiated was as palpable and real as gravity. You could feel it; you could almost hold it in your hand. No matter what kind of ugly mood had you by the scruff of the neck, her smile set you free. Grandma had just finished talking with God and everything was, profoundly, right with the world.

Talking with God

I cannot remember how young I was when I first realized that Grandma said, "talk with God" instead of the usual "talk to God" that most people say when discussing prayer. Indeed, the transformation that would occur within her bespoke of something much more than simply a one-sided long distance conversation. I mean, it looked like she and God had actually been sitting in her room having a chat!

When I asked her what she and God talked about, she would reply, "Oh, all kinds of things." "Big stuff?" I asked. "Yes," she said "but, small things, too. I ask Him to watch over you and the rest of the family. If I have a problem I ask for His help and the strength to take care of it the way that He wants me to. I thank Him for all of the happiness and blessings He has given me. Most of the time, though, God talks and I listen to Him. You have to listen if you're going to have a real conversation with God. He likes it when we listen, just the way I like it when you listen to me. After all, He loves me the way that I love you."

"Do you only talk to God in your room?" I asked. "No," she said. "He meets me here." As she spoke she touched my heart with her hand. "I talk with Him here." That made me feel good and I remember thinking in a child's way that while it was important to love God, it was far more important to let Him love you.

Be joyful always; pray continually; give thanks in all circumstances, for this is God's will for you in Christ Jesus.
—1 Thessalonians 5:16-18

Any Time, Any Place, Any Thing, Any Subject

As I grew older, my fascination with prayer grew, as did my love for God. Yes, our relationship had its rocky moments, but pop culture and arrogant churchmen aside, I never lost contact with Him or forgot how important it was to surrender to His Grace.

Grandma Vi continued to amaze me with her gifts of prayer. When I would drive the twelve hours from college to my grandparents' trailer in Bossier City, Louisiana, she would, quite literally, pray me in. Think about it; she would go about her daily chores with half of her attention actively engaged in a twelve-hour-long continuous prayer for my safe journey. Frequently, she'd have a "message from God" for me when I arrived at the trailer, along with a warm embrace and a home cooked meal that was fit for, well, Jehovah.

Later, when I was rested and ready to drive the additional three hours to home, she would smile and say, "Be careful and be sure to call me when you get to your Mom's house so I know when to quit praying." No matter what time it was, she wouldn't go to sleep until she'd received my call.

I have no doubt that even after I called the trailer to let her know of my safe arrival, she continued to pray. It was clear to me that her whole life was a prayer. That was what I wanted for myself and, over the years, it became what I wanted for everyone else.

Grandma made it plain; a person could—and should—have a heartfelt conversation with God anytime, anywhere, under any circumstances, and about anything.

Different Kinds of Prayer

Grandma's prayers on my behalf were an example of Intercessory prayer, where one person prays for another. There are other kinds of prayer as well.

There are prayers of Thanksgiving and of Praise where we thank our Heavenly Father for the blessings He has given us and give honor to His Grace and Perfect Will. We can obtain more of God through Seeking prayer wherein we simply announce our intention to rest in His presence and allow Him to speak through His Word. Prayers of Confession allow you to repent your sins and ask your Father for the blessing of His forgiveness. Prayers of Supplication involve asking God for His Divine intervention. Submissive prayer or prayers of Surrender involve completely opening up to God's love and welcoming His Grace and Will into our lives.

Different Ways to Pray

Just as there are different kinds of prayer, there are also different ways to pray. You may talk with God silently or aloud. You may mindfully and deliberately repeat passages from the Bible while pondering the meaning of His Word. This is called Repetitive prayer. Prayer can be performed Reflectively by sitting still and coming to know God through the peace of silence or by reflecting on the deeper meaning of His hand at work in your life.

The Most Important Thing about Prayer

Don't let the different kinds of prayer or the different ways to pray confuse you. Remember Grandma Vi's model:

You talk with God (that means listening as well as talking)

- Anytime,
- Anywhere,
- (under) Any circumstances,
- (about) Anything.
- ?

But something is missing. What's vitally important is that your prayers be authentic, that is, they must come from your heart and be in your own voice. Even if you are reading a Biblically based prayer composed by someone else, you must make it real for you. You must see it, feel it, taste it, and touch it with everything you've got. So now we have our final "A": Authentically.

You talk with God

- Anytime
- Anywhere
- Any Circumstances
- Anything
- Authentically

Do not be anxious about anything, but in everything, by prayer and petition, with thanksgiving, present your requests to God. And the peace of God, which transcends all understanding, will guard your hearts and your minds in Christ Jesus.
—*Philippians* 4: 6-7

Call to me and I will answer you and tell you great and unsearchable things you do not know.
—*Jeremiah* 33:3

The Lord is near to all who call on him, to all who call on him in truth.
—*Psalm* 145:18

Why Should Teachers Pray?

There are so many good reasons for teachers to pray. To start with, reread the list on page 19. All of those problems and circumstances can be addressed and solved with prayer. But there are other reasons as well. You can pray:

- for spiritual growth
- for material needs
- for protection from evil
- to confess your sins and ask for forgiveness
- for the sins of others
- for the needs of others
- for the church and its missions
- for others to receive His Word

- for personal healing
- for others to be healed
- for wisdom about any subject
- to help simplify your life
- for personal direction
- to participate in His Holy work around the world

The list could go on forever. When it comes to prayer, you are only as limited as your imagination.

I tell you the truth, my Father will give you whatever you ask in my name. Until now you have not asked for anything in my name. Ask and you will receive, and your joy will be complete.
— *John* 16:23-24

Prayer is a wonderful gift from our Heavenly Father. He places great value on it and we should avail ourselves of it. So much can be accomplished through the power of prayer. You have but to read the stories of Moses, Samson, Elijah, and the apostle Peter in the Bible to grasp its potential.*

Yet, so often, we feel like we don't have the time or the energy for prayer. Many of us lead such busy lives. Our minds and our bodies work overtime to accomplish the many things we must in order to fulfill our earthly obligations. But when we stop to pray, even if only for a few moments, our whole being changes. We slow our frantic pace, focus on God, and say, "Lord, I love you with all my heart and soul."

Whenever anyone asks me why they should pray, rather than listing the reasons, I say this: "Your Heavenly Father loves you dearly and wants you to visit with Him often. He wants you to come to Him for rest, advice, encouragement, and all manner of council. You can visit anytime you want, day or night. Calling ahead isn't necessary because He is always home waiting for you, His beloved child. There amid the beats of His heart, you will surely find nourishment, comfort, and joy. You will find meaning and direction. If you come to Him when you are sick, He will heal you. No matter how many people are cruel to you or how much life has beaten you down, you can always go to your Father's home. You can tell Him anything and He will be there for you. All you have to do is show up. The doorway to His heart is His son Jesus Christ and the key to that doorway is prayer." Now that sounds like reason enough for me. How about you?

*Moses (Exodus 15:24-26); Samson (Judges 16:28-30); Elijah (James 5:17,18); Peter (Acts 9:36-41).

One of those days Jesus went out to a mountainside to pray, and spent the night praying to God.
—Luke 6:12

But Jesus often withdrew to lonely places and prayed.
—Luke 5:16

Very early in the morning, while it was still dark, Jesus got up, left the house and went off to a solitary place, where he prayed.
—Mark 1:35

How-to for Teachers

But when you pray, go into your room, close the door and pray to your Father, who is unseen. Then your Father, who sees what is done in secret, will reward you.
—*Matthew* 6:6

Step One:
Set the Stage with Solitude, Silence, and Stillness

Do you remember how Grandma Vi would go into her room to pray? She was following the instructions laid out in Matthew 6:6. It's the very first thing you should do before you pray: find a place of solitude and enter it.

Your place of solitude can be a room or the corner of a room. It can be your back porch. In truth, it doesn't even have to be a physical structure. It can even be in a classroom filled with children. It can be any place where you can engineer a feeling of being alone.

When you enter into solitude you enter into the realm of the soul. Here, God gives you the opportunity to drop all pretense and be yourself. When you are in solitude you are never really alone. You and your Heavenly Father are there together. That is His promise.

After entering into the realm of the soul, you should then embrace silence and stillness. Here's how you do it.

Generally relax, accept the guidance of the Holy Spirit and tell yourself that you are preparing for prayer, preparing to talk with God. Close your eyes and briefly watch your body and how it naturally moves. For example, your chest rises and falls as you breathe. That's okay; just let it. Perhaps you notice some tension in your neck so you gently drop your shoulders downward a bit to release it. If you notice any physical movement at all, just take notice of it and say to yourself that you'd like to sit as still as you are comfortably able.

Turn your attention to your mind. Other than focusing on God and your intention to pray, don't try to control it in any way. Try not to chastise yourself for a wandering mind that jumps around in the background from one mental topic to the next. Simply acknowledge that your mind is doing something, casually watch it unfold, and keep your focus on your Father and His presence.

You may find it helpful, as opportunity allows, to have soothing music accompany your preparations for prayer. If so, you will enjoy the Morning Cup Audio CD that accompanies this volume. It was designed especially to set the tone for your prayer time.

Settling into a time of prayer is like watching a river flow by out of the corner of your eye. You'll notice obvious things like a child doing his or her work, or perhaps children enjoying recreation in the schoolyard. You're sitting in one place with God but all of the life and energy of children move before you. Enjoy yourself. After all, you are preparing to talk with God. What could be better than that?

Put a light smile on your face as you allow the river of your mind to float by and you'll begin to notice something: your mind will settle down, your body will relax, and you will begin to feel quiet all over. Sometimes it feels as if you are sensing all of your parts all at once. The best word I know of to describe your sensation is "quiescence." Every part of you settles down and you will feel organized and peaceful. You become bathed in God's Grace and Presence. Now you are ready. This is the canvas upon which you will present your prayers.

It Only Takes a Moment

Though you could spend a lot of time completing your preparations for prayer, it really only takes a moment to engineer solitude, silence, and stillness. With practice you'll be able to set the stage for prayer in an instant.

There is benefit in setting the stage and resting in the realm of the soul for longer periods of time. In this way you utilize solitude, silence, and stillness to reflect and listen for God's wisdom and guidance. There in His loving embrace, you will experience genuine tranquility and perfect peace of mind.

Step Two: Embrace a Prayerful Attitude

Prayer is so very much more than mere words. It is an attitude that reflects our most heartfelt wishes and hopes. In reality, it's all about heart—your heart to God's heart.

We are all God's children. As a parent He isn't gruff or unfeeling, yet we often approach Him as if He is. Our Father is love itself and the secret to true prayer is simple: we must be His children.

I often ask people who pray regularly to listen to themselves as they pray. "Try it for yourself," I say. "How do you sound when you pray? Do you sound like an outsider intruding upon God's quiet repose? Do you plead or beg? Do your words impose or do you sound like a child talking with a beloved parent?"

That last example, of course, is how it should be. We should not sound like spiritual panhandlers. We are God's loving and obedient children and behaving in that way is the secret key to true and authentic prayer.

Every Teacher Is Unique

In His wisdom, our Heavenly Father created each of us to be a unique individual. When He gave us the gift of prayer He knew that each of us would have our own unique way of speaking with Him. That's precisely the way He wants it. He wants each of us to be completely honest and authentic by expressing what's in our heart to Him. Remember, whether you offer spontaneous prayers or prayers composed by someone else, you must feel it in your heart.

Step Three:
Choose Your Method of Prayer

There are many ways that a teacher can pray. For this Morning Cup I've chosen four ways that you may engage in prayer:

Spoken Prayer

Simply put, speak aloud. Declaiming your prayers out loud has a special quality to it. When you taste what you are saying, the words have a greater effect upon you and your prayers become powerful.

Silent Prayer

Silent prayers are more intimate than spoken ones. Praying in this way brings a delicate and private quality to your worship. Use silent prayer whenever you feel the need to more personally connect with your Heavenly Father.

Repetitive Prayer

Repeat your prayer over and over. You may do this aloud or silently in your mind. However, no matter how you choose to say the prayer, it is important that each repetition be mindful and deliberate. Mindlessly repeating words is not praying. Repetitive, authentic prayer produces a profoundly focused communication with God.

Reflective Prayer

Reflective prayer is performed in silence. Simply read a Biblical passage or any prayer that you choose and silently reflect on its meaning. Just hold the thought of the prayer in your heart and mind. The Holy Spirit does the rest. Reflective prayer engenders peaceful communication with God and reveals His Wisdom.

Step Four: Talk with God

All of the prayers that make up the balance of this book have been composed, and the Bible selections chosen, with the idea of using them in any one of the above prayer methods outlined in Step Three. Of course, you can dispense with them altogether and speak with your Father according to the dictates of your heart. But what if you have never prayed before?

Do you remember my comments in the beginning about teachers who say that they don't know how to pray? All too often, they really just don't know what to say to God. If you are one of those people then you probably remember that I also told you not to worry.

The next section of this book contains all the suggestions you need to learn how to speak the language of prayer. Please learn from it and let it inspire you to lead a prayerful life. Your Father is in His home and He would dearly love to speak with you.

Step Five: Listen to God

The fifth and final step of prayer is probably the most important. At least it was for Grandma Vi. Do you remember what she said about how she spent most of her prayer time? That's right; she spent it listening.

Please remember, authentic prayer is a conversation filled with devotion and love that takes place between you and your Heavenly Father. Prayer is so incredibly precious to God. It releases an enormous outpouring of His wisdom, power, inspiration, and strength. But you have to listen and you have to listen patiently.

After speaking to Him, ask God to speak back to you in any way He sees fit. You may use the journal that begins on page 71 to record any important thoughts and insights that come up, especially when He speaks to you through His Word. Let Him call your attention to those areas in your life where He wants to help.

Spend as much time listening to God as you would like. One minute of really listening to God would be great. Fifteen would be so much better. You choose. An hour listening to God isn't too much, and neither is a lifetime.

Let us then labor for an inward stillness,
An inward stillness and an inward healing;
That perfect silence where lips and heart
Are still, and we no longer entertain
Our own imperfect thoughts and vain opinions,
But God alone speaks in us, and we wait
In singleness of heart, that we may know
God's will, and in the silence of our spirit,
That we may do God's will and do that only.
—Longfellow, The Christus

A Teacher's Life Inspired by Prayer

I've always loved the word "inspired." It means, "in-spirit." When my publisher approached me to write several books on prayer for the Morning Cup series she could hardly have known that on those mornings after my Grandmother had chatted with God, she would, invariably, make a cup of tea, sit down, leisurely sip, and bask in the glow of being "in spirit." I can think of no better way to start a day or spend a life. Can you?

The Lord's Prayer

This, then, is how you should pray:
"Our Father in heaven,
hallowed be your name,

your kingdom come,
your will be done
on earth as it is in heaven.

Give us today our daily bread.
Forgive us our debts,
as we also have forgiven our debtors.

And lead us not into temptation,
but deliver us from the evil one."
—Matthew 6:9-13

Prayers for Teachers

Whenever the demands of being a teacher make you feel tense, nervous, and uncertain, it is time to surrender through prayer. Authentic prayer is a fundamental rededication of your faith every time you engage in it. It brings the peace of the Father to you by helping you to completely open up to His love, wisdom, strength, and forgiveness.

Relax your heart and bring peace to your soul by surrendering all of your cares and worries to God through prayer. What doubts could you possibly have when you are resting in your Father's loving arms while being filled with His Grace?

Prayers

As you begin to incorporate prayer into your life, you may find it helpful to have examples of prayers to get you started. Here are some samples that, along with selected scripture passages, will set the tone for prayer. As you make these initial steps, the Holy Spirit will help you in your efforts.

A Prayer of Surrender

Father, in the name of Jesus, I surrender to the Holy Spirit. Fill my soul with Your Grace and let me lead the life that You have set out for me as a teacher. Amen.

That if you confess with your mouth, "Jesus is Lord," and believe in your heart that God raised him from the dead, you will be saved. For it is with your heart that you believe and are justified, and it is with your mouth that you confess and are saved.

—Romans 10:9-10

... if my people, who are called by my name, will humble themselves and pray and seek my face and turn from their wicked ways, then will I hear from heaven and will forgive their sin and will heal their land.
—2 Chronicles 7:14

A Prayer for Wisdom

Father, I stand before the Throne fully open to receive Your wisdom. I surrender to Your instruction and rest peacefully without fear. Today I accept the guidance of Your wisdom revealed to me through insight and understanding. In Jesus' name, Amen.

If any of you lacks wisdom, he should ask God, who gives generously to all without finding fault, and it will be given to him. But when he asks, he must believe and not doubt, because he who doubts is like a wave of the sea, blown and tossed by the wind.
—James 1:5-6

. . . turning your ear to wisdom
and applying your heart to understanding,
—Proverbs 2:2

For God so loved the world that he gave his one and only Son, that whoever believes in him shall not perish but have eternal life.
— John 3:16

A Prayer for Safekeeping

Lord above, I know that You are constantly watching over me. I invite Your care and Heavenly gaze. Please watch over me as I watch over my students and charges. Father, let Your Grace flow through me to them. In Jesus' Name I pray, Amen.

For lack of guidance a nation falls,
but many advisers make victory sure.
—Proverbs 11:14

The true light that gives light to every man was coming into the world.
—John 1:9

A Prayer for Unity

Heavenly Father, please give me the strength to avoid gossiping about and criticizing my teaching colleagues. Help me to remember that we all behave in accordance with the gifts You have given us. For our students' sakes, it is so important that we get along and work well together. With Your strength and the gift of the Holy Spirit to guide me, I know I can overcome my weaknesses. Amen.

Who are you to judge someone else's servant? To his own master he stands or falls. And he will stand, for the Lord is able to make him stand.
—Romans 14:4

A wicked man listens to evil lips;
a liar pays attention to a malicious tongue.
—Proverbs 17:4

You, then, why do you judge your brother? Or why do you look down on your brother? For we will all stand before God's judgment seat.
—Romans 14:10

A Prayer for Discernment

Dearest Lord, help me to always recognize the needs of my students and to come to their aid according to Your Word. Amen.

From heaven the LORD looks down
and sees all mankind;

from his dwelling place he watches
all who live on earth—

he who forms the hearts of all,
who considers everything they do.
—Psalm 33:13-15

A Prayer for Guidance

Father, You know that parents love their children just as You love us. It is hard for parents to hear troubling things about their children. Some things they may not want to know. Help me to wisely counsel parents so that they may learn to better shape and mold the lives of their children. Amen.

You guide me with your counsel, and afterward you will take me into glory.
—Psalm 73:24

... let the wise listen and add to their learning, and let the discerning get guidance.
—Proverbs 1:5

A Prayer for Direction

Heavenly Father, I come to You in the name of Jesus because one of my students is in great peril. I know that I must intervene, but I need Your wisdom and strength if I am to succeed. Through Your Holy Word, guide my actions in the days to come and watch over all those involved. Amen.

Do not merely listen to the word, and so deceive yourselves. Do what it says.
—*James* 1:22

and you have been given fullness in Christ, who is the head over every power and authority.
—Colossians 2:10

A Prayer for Patience

Lord, help me to remember that each student is unique, has meaning, and learns differently. In Your Spirit, I will remember that the most difficult students are the ones who need the most patience, attention, and love. Watch over me Father, and help me to show the same kind of patience for my unique students, that You show for me. Amen.

And we pray this in order that you may live a life worthy of the Lord and may please him in every way: bearing fruit in every good work, growing in the knowledge of God, being strengthened with all power according to his glorious might so that you may have great endurance and patience, and joyfully giving thanks to the Father, who has qualified you to share in the inheritance of the saints in the Kingdom of light.
—*Colossians* 1:10-12

A Prayer of Thanks

Heavenly Father, I have so much to be thankful for because You have given me so much. As a teacher and Your devoted child:

Thank You for the opportunity to touch so many lives.

Thank You for the ability to keep learning more about the gift of the world.

Thank You for administrators and staff who make my job easier.

Thank You for all the little things my students do for me.

Thank You for summer vacation so I can rest and rejuvenate.

Thank You for the wonder of the first day of school with all its freshness and excitement.

Thank You for the gift of watching my students graduate and move to the next chapter of Your plan.

Thank You for the light in my students' eyes when they understand something new.

But, most of all,

Thank You for making me a teacher and guiding me to my calling.

In Jesus' Name I pray, Amen.

An Extra Sip

Prayerwalking

Whenever you've had a busy day at school, and you feel the pace of life start to run over you, it's time for walking prayers or Prayerwalking.

Every time you take a step you have the opportunity for prayer. In many ways, walking prayers can have more impact on you than standing, kneeling, or sitting while you pray. This is because your entire body is in motion when you walk just as it is when you are going about your daily tasks. It is instrumental in teaching you how to pray during any activity and, eventually, to pray without ceasing.

Prayerwalking intrinsically reminds us of our connection to God's miracle, that is the earth. When we walk we feel it beneath our feet. We know it with our whole body just as we know about our Heavenly connection to our Father through our souls. Walking prayers enliven your senses, clear your thinking, and can energize you to God's Word. If you ever need reaffirmation of your chosen path in life or if you are having a hard time standing your ground for what you believe in, then pray as you walk.

Walking prayers are best done when you are alone. Anywhere you can walk slowly and deliberately will be suitable for these prayers. I prefer the outdoors, be it a city park, the woods, or your backyard. The choice is yours. It is important to bring a sense of stillness to your walk.

Pretend that the prayers are delicate and that a hurried pace might break them. Be gentle with yourself. As you walk among the many gifts that He has placed for us in this world, know that each step you take brings you closer to Him.

If you choose to walk in a public place, be sure not to call attention to what you are doing. But take the opportunity to pray for people you see along the way. If you pass someone who is obviously ill, then pray for them. If you see someone giving into sin, pray for their deliverance. You can walk around your home, garden, campus, or city hall and bring the power of prayer with you everywhere. Simply, walk and talk with God.

Walking Prayers

I walk with God in peace and contentment.
I walk with God and recognize His gifts to
me.
I walk with God and am nourished by His
loving kindness.
I walk with God and am healed and
strengthened by His Grace.
I walk with God and extend His love to
everyone.
I walk with God knowing that He is with me
always.
I walk with God and am filled with the Holy
Spirit.
I walk with God and breathe in His mercy.
I walk with God knowing His Perfect Will.
I walk with God upon a bedrock of His Word
and bring the light of His message to the
world.
In Jesus' name I pray, Amen.

For you have delivered me from death
and my feet from stumbling,
that I may walk before God
in the light of life.
—Psalm 56:13

A Prayer for Renewal

Heavenly Father, let each step I take remind me that the Holy Spirit rests with me as I, in turn, rest with the Spirit. Each step enlivens and regenerates me, even in the presence of my enemies. The Spirit erases confusion and helps me to walk away from evil. It unerringly guides me to your goodness. Amen.

He will cover you with his feathers,
and under his wings you will find refuge;
his faithfulness will be your shield and rampart.
—Psalm 91:4

But when he, the Spirit of truth, comes, he will guide you into all truth. He will not speak on his own; he will speak only what he hears, and he will tell you what is yet to come.
—John 16:13

An Affirmation

Every step that I take is a step of happiness.
Every step that I take reaffirms Your Word.
Every step that I take fills me with joy
Because I am walking in Your miracle.

Commit your way to the LORD;
trust in him and he will do this...
—Psalm 37:5

A Prayer for Compliance

Father, place in me Your wishes and desires. As I walk I will listen with my heart and follow Your directions; for I know that Your Divine Will is my chosen path. Amen.

For the eyes of the Lord are on the righteous
and his ears are attentive to their prayer,
but the face of the Lord is against those who do evil.
—1 Peter 3:12

A Prayer for Knowledge

Heavenly Father, help me to walk in Your Word and know Your way.

We demolish arguments and every pretension that sets itself up against the knowledge of God, and we take captive every thought to make it obedient to Christ.
—2 Corinthians 10:5

An Affirmation of Love

Every step I take is taken in complete love: the love of God.

A Teacher's Prayer Journal

Have you ever wondered whether there is more spiritual life than you are currently experiencing? For most, the answer is usually, "Yes." It is perfectly fine and, I think, natural to expect something deeper, richer, and more profound from your spiritual life and a more complete experience of prayer is the key to realizing it.

Use these pages to keep a journal about your new life of prayer. Write down whom or what you are praying for and use it as both a reminder and a way to stay on a prayerful track.

"I have been driven many times to my knees by the overwhelming conviction that I had nowhere else to go."

Abraham Lincoln

"Prayer is the language of a man burdened with a sense of need."

E.M. Bounds

"We have to pray with our eyes on God, not on the difficulties."

Oswald Chambers

"Prayer is not merely an occasional impulse to which we respond when we are in trouble: prayer is a life attitude."

Walter A. Mueller

About the Author

John Bright-Fey teaches classes on prayer, contemplation, and leading a prayerful life. He is the author of several books in the Morning Cup and Whole Heart series. He lives in Birmingham, Alabama.

You may also enjoy these other devotionals in the Morning Cup series. Each one would be a welcomed and treasured gift for the special people in your life.

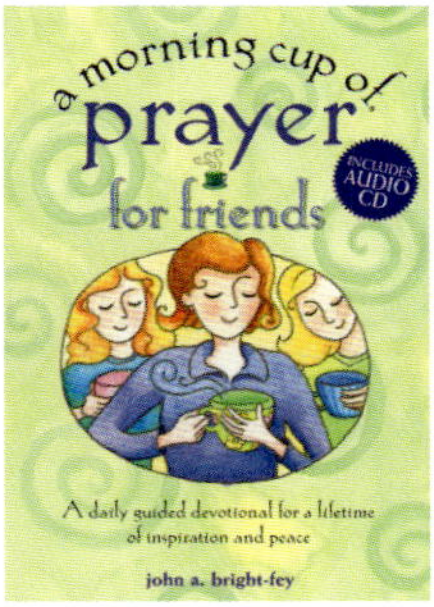

A Morning Cup of® Prayer for Friends

ISBN-13: 978-1-58173-599-4
ISBN-10: 1-58173-599-5

A Morning Cup of® Prayer for Mothers

ISBN-13: 978-1-58173-598-7
ISBN-10: 1-58173-598-7

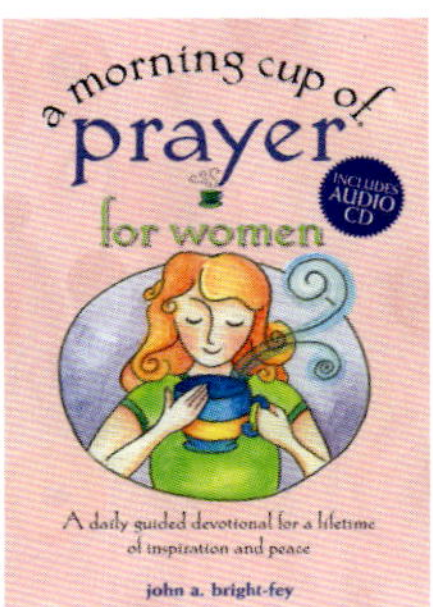

A Morning Cup of® Prayer for Women

ISBN-13: 978-1-58173-596-3
ISBN-10: 1-58173-596-0

Prayer at a Glance

Prayer is talking with God

- Anytime
- Anywhere
- Under any circumstance
- About anything
- Authentically

 **Step One:** Set the stage with solitude, silence, and stillness.

 **Step Two:** Embrace a prayerful attitude.

 **Step Three:** Choose your method of prayer.

 **Step Four:** Talk with God.

 **Step Five:** Listen to God.

Tear this page out and post it in a handy spot for quick reference to help you make time to pray.